Visions of the King: *Jesus Revealed*

By Tonja K. Taylor

Also by Tonja K. Taylor

POWERLight Lit Tips for Better Teaching
The New Legacy Expanded
P.O.W.E.R. Princess Poetry Plus
The Adventures of Princess Pearl, P.O.W.E.R. Girl!
Your Holy Health: Effective Secrets to Divine Life
Spirit Songs & Stories Enhanced
Spirit Songs & Stories Enhanced #2
Visions of the King: Jesus Revealed

Watch for more at https://www.faithwriters.com/
member-profile.php?id=64826.

Table of Contents

To King Jesus, Who is my Zoe Life (John 10:10)!

To my dear husband and all who have prayed and encouraged me through the years to communicate God's Word in creative ways, that all may know Him!

"For just as through the disobedience of the one man the many were made sinners, <u>so also through the obedience of the one man the many will be made righteous."</u> - Romans 5:19, Berean Standard Bible (underline emphasis mine)

Blessed are the pure in heart, for they will see God. - Matthew 5:8, Berean Standard Bible

16 He held in His right hand seven stars, and a sharp double-edged sword came from His mouth. His face was like the sun shining at its brightest. 17 When I saw Him, I fell at His feet like a dead man. But He placed His right hand on me and said, "Do not be afraid. I am the First and the Last, 18 the Living One. I was dead, and behold, now I am alive forever and ever! And I hold the keys of Death and of Hades. - Revelation 1:16-18, Berean Standard Bible

ISBN ebook: 978-1-965641-33-0
ISBN print: 978-1-965641-34-7

All Scripture quotations are from The Berean Standard Bible.

For tips on victorious living in many areas of life, and **soul-strengthening reads**, check out Tonja's 1,500+ articles, stories, poems, and songs at FaithWriters:

https://www.faithwriters.com/member-profile.php?id=64826

Check out our You Tube channels: "River Rain Creative" **https://www.youtube.com/@riverraincreative599/videos,**

and "**POWERLight Learning**": **https://www.youtube.com/@POWERLightLearning-qu7tn/ videos**

It is our prayer that the real and wonderful Savior, Jesus Christ, will be revealed to you in a deeper way as you read these works!

Welcome to the Royal Family!

KING JESUS WILL SOON return to earth, to take us who believe in Him back to Heaven (Revelation 22:12)!

It's not going to be long; many experts believe He will return while you and I are alive!

He will be coming back to get all who believe in Him, to take them back to Heaven to live with Him for eternity!

He wants to be your BFF—Best Friend Forever—and take you with Him to Paradise, where there is freedom and joy and plenty of every good and beautiful thing—and where there are no bad things, no scary things; no darkness at all.

Spirits live forever, and Jesus created you as a spirit who lives in a body (until your body dies), so you are already going to live forever. The choice is yours whether you live with Him in Paradise, or forever separated from Him in hell.

Every good thing in your life is from GOD, Who loves you so much that He sent Jesus (His only Son, The King!) to die for you. Jesus took everything you've ever done wrong and paid for your debt of sin by dying for you on the cross (John 3:15-17).

None of us can get into Heaven to live with God the Father unless we become friends with Jesus, God's Son. When we ask Jesus into our hearts, God adopts us as His kids (John 1:13 and I John 3:1) Then Jesus is our Brother and Savior, and talks to God to help Him remember that the blood He shed for us on the cross is the sacrifice that pays for our sins, and cleanses us.

After Christ Jesus was dead three days, He rose again, and He lives forever! He wants you and every person to be in His Family. You just say, "Yes" to Him—and you'll get the life in Heaven—getting to know Him now, as you learn how to have a great life here.

The moment you say "Yes!" to Jesus, the only Savior of the world, you get a perfect, beautiful new robe to wear—so that when God sees you, you look just like His Son!

Then God the Father is smiling at us and we have an eternal Covenant with Him that provides protection, peace, abundance, success, freedom, and much more (Psalm 89:34, Romans 9:25)!

If you would like to go to Heaven and have Jesus as your BFF, just say this prayer:

Dear Jesus,

Please forgive me of everything I've done wrong and come into my heart and be my LORD and Savior and Friend. Help me get to know You and teach me through Your Word how to love and obey You, for You are the true King Who rules! I renounce every way and work of darkness in my life, now. Thank You for loving me so much. Thank You for saving me and helping me to enjoy and love and live for You! In Your Name, amen!

Romans 10:9 says that if you will **confess** the LORD Jesus with your mouth and **believe** that God raised Him from the dead, then you will be saved (born again; be regenerated in your spirit).

Romans 10:13 says, **"All who call upon the Name of the LORD shall be saved."** When you prayed this prayer, a miracle just happened—you became Jesus' friend, and God's child! The Holy Spirit also came and put a Heavenly mark on you to tell God and the angels and the devil and everyone else that you now belong to Jesus! He will love and help you forever.

Just think—Jesus and His angels are having a party for your most excellent choice (Luke 15:10)!

The way to learn all about your new Best Friend Forever is to read your Bible—His special Letter to you—and ask Him to lead you to the right church family, where you can learn more about Jesus, and meet other brothers and sisters in Christ.

He will also teach you to worship Him in music, and to pray to Him every day, which means to talk to Him and listen to Him, just like you do with your other loved ones!

Welcome to the Royal Family!

3 Ways to Bring Heaven to Earth
Reprinted from FaithWriters.com

(NOTE FROM TONJA: THE LORD Jesus—the only Savior of the world—wants to communicate with you more deeply. Truly, the things of the Spirit are more real than the things of earth, which is passing away!)

"Heaven on earth" is the Presence of God, Who is Love (I John 4:8). Love is what we are created to experience, and the most we experience God, the more we understand and enjoy Love!

Who (what true Believer in Jesus Christ, who is actively following Him) does not want a Heavenly life?

The LORD makes it easy (which was always His plan, staring with the Garden of Eden in Genesis 1!) for us to have days of Heaven upon earth—a taste of what it will be like when we are with Him forever in Heaven! Hallelujah!

When the LORD draws us by His Spirit and brings us to saving faith in the LORD Jesus Christ, during which we realize our sin and deep need to be forgiven and cleansed by the blood of Jesus, then we receive Christ Jesus as our Savior and LORD (John 3:14-17).

We are sealed for Heaven by the Holy Spirit, and Christ Jesus—the Essence of Heaven!—comes into our hearts to live with us forever.

And now He has revealed this grace through the appearing of our Savior, Christ Jesus, who has abolished death and illuminated the way to life and immortality through the gospel. - II Timothy 1:10

Praise God! King Jesus has conquered death and given us life through His blood!

21 Now it is God who establishes both us and you in Christ. He anointed us, 22 placed His seal on us, and put His Spirit in our hearts as a pledge of what is to come. II Corinthians 1:21-22

Hallelujah! The Holy Spirit in our hearts is the Guarantee that, when we continue to follow Him and our bodies die, or King Jesus returns, we will go forever to live with Him in Heaven!

Here are three ways that can definitely help you experience more of Heaven on earth:

> Read and study, speak, and memorize God's Word.

18 Fix those words of mine in your hearts and minds; tie them as reminders on your hands and bind them on your foreheads. 19 Teach them to your children, speaking about them when you sit at home and when you walk along the road, when you lie down and when you get up. 20 Write them on the doorposts of your houses and on your gates, 21 so that as long as the heavens are above the earth, your days and those of your children may be multiplied in the land that the LORD swore to give your fathers.—Deuteronomy 11:18-21, Berean Study Bible

> Worship the LORD. Ultimately, this means in every area of life—to use the wisdom He gives us (His Word!) to consecrate ourselves to His will and His way—which is, of course, the very best life for us, His kids; which brings honor and blessing and abundance!

17 I love those who love me, and those who seek me early shall find me. 18 With me are riches and honor, enduring wealth and righteousness. 19 My fruit is better than gold, pure gold, and my harvest surpasses choice silver. - Proverbs 8:17-18

He is the God of Heaven and earth (Gen. 1); our Father Who has adopted us on purpose, to lavish His Love on us for eternity!

Hallelujah!

"O LORD, God of Israel, there is no God like You in heaven or on earth, keeping Your covenant of loving devotion with Your

servants who walk before You with all their hearts. —2 Corinthians 6:14

God is Covenant; He never breaks a promise! We may not believe nor receive what He's done, but He always does His part!

"God is Spirit, and His worshipers must worship Him in spirit and in truth." - John 4:24

"in spirit" means from our hearts; genuine adoration and reverence for the LORD.

4 But when the time had fully come, God sent His Son, born of a woman, born under the law, 5 to redeem those under the law, that we might receive our adoption as sons. 6 And because you are sons, God sent the Spirit of His Son into our hearts, crying out, "Abba, Father!". Galatians 4:4-6

Hallelujah! When we receive Christ Jesus, God's Son, as our Savior and LORD, then Jesus becomes our Big Brother, and we become God's children!

> Praise Him and be thankful for all of His goodness—all the days of your life!

The LORD deserves and honors our appreciation of Him. He alone is worthy of the highest praise! Also, of course, it's a win-win; when we praise the LORD, our minds are set on Him and positives, and we feel better—which is part of Heaven on earth!

4 Enter His gates with thanksgiving and His courts with praise; give thanks to Him and bless His name. 5 For the LORD is good, and His loving devotion endures forever; His faithfulness continues to all generations.--Psalm 100:4-5

If we praised and worshiped Him 24/7, He would still deserve more! Every moment and molecule of any good in our lives is from Him, our dear Father, in Whom is no darkness at all, nor turning from pure Light (I John 1:5)!

17 Pray without ceasing. 18 Give thanks in every circumstance, for this is God's will for you in Christ Jesus. 19 Do not extinguish the Spirit...—I Thessalonians 5:17-19

Prayer is, at its core, simply communicating with God; in our hearts and minds, and/or out loud.

God is holy, but through the blood of the LORD Jesus Christ that covers us when we receive Him as LORD and Savior, we can approach the One Who lives in unapproachable Light (I Tim 6:13-16)!

Yet You are holy, enthroned on the praises of Israel.– Psalm 22:3

So enjoy more of Heaven on earth from now on—and *teach others how!*

Chapter 1: His Love Makes Us One

1 Behold what manner of love the Father has given to us, that we should be called children of God. And that is what we are! The reason the world does not know us is that is did not know Him. 2 Beloved, we are now children of God, and what we will be has not yet been revealed. We know that when Christ appears, we will be like Him, for we will see Him as He is. – I John 3:1-2

MAY 28, 2006: AS USUAL, my husband and I met to pray this morning with the warriors at church. While our worship team practiced in the background to spirit-stirring songs, the Lord gave me a wonderful vision.

I was in the throne room of God, and there sat His Majesty on the throne, with the Lord Jesus Christ at His right hand. The thrones were encircled with a rainbow, and there were angels everywhere, some standing and worshipping, some flying around His head.

I was clothed in white garments, crawling at first, bowing before the throne of the awesome God. Then suddenly, I was lifted up and into the open arms and lap of my loving Father! He drew me to His bosom and held me tight, enfolding me in His garments of light. I was completely hidden in Him.

Then, again I know not how, I was not in His arms any longer. He had given me many crowns, and somehow I gave them to Jesus – not throwing them and not handing them to Him, but I presented them to Him; and He, the King of Glory, the Righteousness of God, accepted them.

Then I saw His beautiful smile. He looked into my eyes and held out His hand. He pointed to His palm.

"See?" He said. "I have engraved you in the palm of My hand."

There, in glistening red cursive, was <u>my name; literally engraved – cut into! – His palm!</u>

As Isaiah 49:15 and 16 says, **Can a woman forget her nursing child, or lack compassion for the son of her womb? Though she may forget, I will not forget you! Behold, I have inscribed you on the palms of My hands; your walls are ever before Me.**

After that, He lifted me up and into His arms, and pulled me to Himself as His Father had, and lovingly embraced me, so closely that it seemed I melted into Him, that we became one!

My Savior and I exulted together and the peace and joy I felt were so inexpressible, so deep!

And in all of this, I could only think, WOW! Even the angels, as pure and completely devoted as they are, have not, cannot, could never experience this! For this is the love of a Savior for the one on whom He has had mercy; this is the agape love of a Father for His child.

◦◦◦◦◦◦

THERE ARE MANY PROOFS in our lives every day that the LORD loves us. What are three things you can think of immediately, that are proof that the LORD God loves you?

Chapter 2: Jesus is the Sword of the Word

And take the helmet of salvation and the sword of the Spirit, which is the word of God. – Ephesians 6:17

YEARS AGO, I HAD THIS vision (some would call it a dream): I am standing in a field, with nothing and no one close around me. I have a Bible and it is open, and I'm reading from it. My right pointer finger is tracing the lines of Scripture as I say them out loud.

Suddenly, the hand of Jesus—the Living Word!-reaches up out of the pages and grabs mine!

I am delighted! I keep pulling, and Jesus Himself rises up out of the Holy Book, manifesting until He stands beside me! He is smiling, and so am I.

"Teach me, Jesus!" I say.

And He does!

His Word is alive!

ASK HIM, AND HE WILL help you understand His Word more than ever, and wield it as a victorious sword against the enemy—and for your abundant (Zoe; John 10:10) life!

Chapter 3: The Secret Place

1 **He who dwells in the shelter of the Most High Will abide in the shadow of the Almighty. 2 I will say to the LORD, "My refuge and my fortress, My God, in whom I trust!"** - Psalm 91:1-2

IN MY VISION, I AM a child on Jesus' lap. He is dressed in white robes. I am facing Him.

Smiling, He pulls His train (attached to His crown, touching the floor and flowing outward, like the long train on a bridal dress) around us to totally enclose us.

Then a whole new dimension—*The Secret Place!*—opens up!

We are outside in such a beautiful, pristine place; and there, He tells me secrets...

This most intimate time with the LORD Jesus Christ is available to those who fear, revere, and worship Him! As children of God who have received Christ Jesus as Savior and LORD by believing in His atoning death through His pure blood, shed on the cross, we have the privilege to communicate with the Creator and Sustainer of all Life and the universe!

If you have not been born again and want to receive Christ Jesus as your Savior, LORD, and Best Friend forever (He will never leave you nor forsake you! Hebrews 13:5), please say the prayer at the front of this book.

Now, *congratulations!* If you just said that prayer and meant it, you are truly born again! God is now your loving Father, Jesus is your Brother Who and Good Shepherd who will always be with you and will lead you in right paths, and the angels are having a party to celebrate your most excellent decision! Your spirit has been translated from the temporary kingdom of darkness into the eternal Kingdom of Light of God's dear Son, King Jesus!

Ask the LORD to show you the right church body for you to become part of, and for the right Bible to study. Remember there are multiple versions and languages online to use. He will give you help you by giving you His wisdom, favor, strength, and grace! He loves you so very much!

If you are not aware of The Secret Place with God, you can start cultivating it today: Turn off all the electronics and the radio, and get in a quiet place, away from other people and noise, as much as possible. (Sometimes I have just sat in my car with the windows up, to be quiet and alone for a bit.)

Welcome the Holy Spirit and ask Him to help you hear what He is already saying. You may want to worship by singing quietly to Him, or pray, and/or read His Word.

Ask Him to help you focus on Him, on things above.

It helps me to look up at the sky, and just start thanking Him that He is with me, even though I may not feel Him. He is a Person Who loves you and wants to talk to you. Soon, you will get a thought or impression. When God speaks, it will bring peace, even if it is a warning or conviction.

The more you practice being in The Secret Place with Him, the more easily you will be able to enter into it, and understand His way!

Chapter 4: I Love Jehovah Nissi, My Defender

But the Lord your God you shall [reverently] fear; then He will deliver you out of the hands of all your enemies. - 2 Kings 17:39, AMPC

1 He who dwells in the shelter of the Most High Will abide in the shadow of the Almighty. 2 I will say to the LORD, "My refuge and my fortress, My God, in whom I trust!" – Psalm 91:1-2

THIS IS ONE OF THE many visions God has given me of my Savior and Help and Shield and Rock, the LORD Jesus Christ! One of His many names (Many names, but one God! Isaiah 44:8; Isaiah 45:18; Deuteronomy 6:4; Malachi 2:10, James 2:19; Mark 12:29) is Jehovah Nissi. **"And Moses built an altar and named it The LORD Is My Banner."** - Exodus 17:15

In my vision: At first, I am tiny, on the ground with a dozen or so other people, and we are milling around in front of Jesus—Jehovah Nissi—who is standing behind us in brown leather battle gear, with His shining sword drawn.

We are in a clearing in a wooded area somewhere. Suddenly, I am just overwhelmed with thankfulness, knowing He has (literally!) got my back and is protecting me from the enemy. I just have to express my thanks to Him!

Still tiny, I run up His leg and up onto His right shoulder, and I stretch my (very little, compared to Him!) arms as wide as I can across

14

His cheek. He is so big that His cheek is wider than my arms can reach! I just hug Him as much as I can to say *"Thank You my LORD!"*

My truly awesome LORD turns His (huge) head and looks down at me in such love with His big brown (in this vision) right eye, and a huge tear falls from His eye and envelopes me! I am in bliss; totally safe and secure and loved!

The LORD is my rock, my fortress, and my deliverer. My God is my rock, in whom I take refuge, my shield, and the horn of my salvation, my stronghold. - Psalm 18:2

Thank the LORD that, even though you may not have been aware of it, He has protected you from many dangers, all of your life—even when you were in the womb!

If it were not for the LORD's protection and mercy, we would all have been dead and in hell a long time ago!

As He showed me one day years ago, He Who never slumbers nor sleeps has His angels watching over us while we sleep (and the rest of the time), protecting us. He has protected us from more than we can understand, and we may learn all of that in Heaven. Right now, we can just start thanking Him for His constant protection.

Even when we have broken spiritual and physical laws, the LORD has mercy and protects us as much as He can! Hallelujah! Great is His faithfulness, forever!

Chapter 5: The Firstborn of Many Sons

17 **He is before all things, and in Him all things hold together.**
18 And He is the head of the body, the church; He is the
beginning and firstborn from among the dead, so that in all things
He may have preeminence. 19 For God was pleased to have all His
fullness dwell in Him... - Colossians 1:17-19

(THIS WAS A VISION I had while listening to a pastor's wife sing (What an anointed voice!) at a prophetic meeting years ago.)

AS THE PASTOR'S WIFE sang, I could sense the true worship in her heart. Suddenly, I had a vision; the LORD Jesus was on the cross.

I did not see the other two crosses, and this seemed to be on a plain or desert area, instead of on a mountain. The perspective was from some distance, but I was seeing the front of the LORD Jesus.

As the pure, redeeming blood of our LORD and Savior flowed from His pierced body and ran down the cross, every drip formed a new babe; a new person was being born from each drop—so there were many, many babies! (This was the end of the vision.)

I was so thankful that I was truly born again by faith in His blood!

I was very thankful that He was training me to help many know the Way to true Life through Jesus Christ, to become a son or daughter of God to have a blessed life now and forever!

The LORD has birthed you through faith (that He gave you!) in the blood of Jesus (that He provided for us all! John 3:14-17). He wants to birth new things through you, that will help you and others to know, experience, and promote Him better, for He wants every person to have Heaven on earth, as much as possible. That was His plan for all, from the beginning (Genesis 1).

Chapter 6: Redeemed and Blessed!

13 Christ redeemed us from the curse of the Law, having become a curse for us—for it is written, "CURSED IS EVERYONE WHO HANGS ON A TREE"— 14 in order that in Christ Jesus the blessing of Abraham might come to the Gentiles, so that we would receive the promise of the Spirit through faith. – Galatians 3:13-14

JESUS AND THE CROSS are transparent, and we see the mighty Hand of God reaching through Him on the cross to smash the enemy; to set people free!

This is what it means to be redeemed from the curse! When sin—which causes the curse—entered the world through Adam and Even when they betrayed God, all people were doomed to go to hell.

Hell is eternal separation from God.

But God sent Jesus at just the proper time, to die on the cross for us after living a sinless life, and shed His pure blood to pay the sin debt for all people for all time (John 3:15-17), that all who believe in and receive what Christ Jesus did for them may be born again and live in Heaven for eternity! *Hallelujah!*

So when we become born again, we are redeemed from every curse and we are also blessed! We have been given all these rights, just like the rights of any country belong to every citizen. But sometimes we have to fight (the devil, who is the enemy, and who is defeated by what Jesus did for us on the cross!) to have and enjoy our rights.

That is where the Word of God comes in. We speak the Word and agree with God. What He says in His Word is Truth. What He says in His Word is how He thinks about us and what Jesus died for us to have, be, and enjoy. GLORY!

The LORD is faithful to watch over His Word to accomplish it (Jeremiah 1:12), and His angels listen to His Word, and go into action on our behalf.

Bless the LORD, all His angels mighty in strength who carry out His word, who hearken to the voice of His command.- Psalm 103:20, AMPC

Hallelujah!

To be redeemed from every curse and blessed beyond measure, you must be born again. Salvation—being born again, regenerated in your spirit; awakened from being spiritually dead, to being truly spiritually alive!—is completely free to us; Jesus paid it all!

Start thanking the LORD, that no matter what your life is like, you have it better than so many people in the earth!

He who sacrifices a thank offering honors Me, and to him who rights his way, I will show the salvation of God. - Psalm 50:23

Start saying every day that God loves you, for He sent Jesus to die and rise again for you (John 3:15-17; Romans 5:6-8). Say that you are Blessed and highly favored.

The more we say something, the more we will believe it, so say what you want, for this is the way God wants.

His angels listen to and help bring His Word to pass in your life!

Chapter 7: Praise Multiplies God's Power

Psalm 34:1-3: **1 I will bless the LORD at all times; His praise shall continually be in my mouth. 2 My soul will make its boast in the LORD; The humble will hear it and rejoice. 3 O magnify the LORD with me, And let us exalt His name together.**

IN MY VISION, JESUS is standing in the midst of a group of worshippers—me and many others. He is much taller than us.

As we worship, He grows bigger, and He goes around and frees groups of worshippers who are bound—in bondage—and who have not been able to truly worship Him.

He strikes His amazing sharp Sword against the chains that have bound them, and they break free, then join our group.

The Power in Him then grows and multiplies, as there are now more worshiping Him.

As our worship—and thus His power—gets stronger, He continues to seek and find other groups of bound worshipers, and sets them free.

They also join our group—and the power multiplies even more!

(This is really the way it works in our natural lives; the spirit world affects the natural world—in powerful and wonderful ways when we praise and worship LORD Jesus, the King of kings and LORD of lords!)

14 Keep this commandment without stain or reproach until the appearance of our Lord Jesus Christ, 15 which the blessed and only Sovereign One—the King of kings and Lord of lords—will bring about in His own time. 16 He alone is immortal and dwells in

unapproachable light. No one has ever seen Him, nor can anyone see Him. To Him be honor and eternal dominion! Amen. – I Timothy 6:14-16

This is the way it really is; as we worship Christ Jesus, He is magnified in our lives and His power can flow much more freely. It is up to us to worship Him if we want His power!

What can you do today to worship Him more?

He who sacrifices a thank offering honors Me, and to him who rights his way, I will show the salvation of God. - Psalm 50:23

Just start praising Him and thanking Him for all the good things in your life—and that He gives you victory in those things that seem to not be right—and that will help Him make them right for you! Hallelujah!

Chapter 8: Mandate

1 **Listen to Me, O islands; pay attention, O distant peoples: The LORD called Me from the womb; from the body of My mother. He named Me. 2He made my mouth like a sharp sword; He hid me in the shadow of His hand. He made me like a polished arrow; He hid me in His quiver. 3He said to Me, "You are My servant, Israel, in whom I will display My glory."** — Isaiah 49:1-3[1]

THIS IS THE VISION I had when my daughter was a young teen:

She and I are in a cave, in catacombs (in some other country besides the United States of America), meeting secretly with a group of believers. The light is dim, but strong enough to see.

Jesus—the Captain of our Salvation, and LORD of the Angel Armies—dressed in white uniform-type clothing, walks in!

He does not speak to anyone, but leads my daughter and I to a mantle over a fireplace, where there are two swords.

He picks up the first sword and I kneel, and He touches me on each shoulder, then places the sword in my hands.

He does the same for my daughter, to whom He gives a smaller sword.

We understand that our mandate ("an official order or commission to do something," per the internet) is that we are to take the Word and

---

1. http://biblia.com/bible/esv/Isaiah%2049.1-3

wield it—against the enemy and to bring healing, freedom, and hope to the world. *Hallelujah!*

15 And He said to them, "Go into all the world and preach the gospel to all creation. 16 "He who has believed and has been baptized shall be saved; but he who has disbelieved shall be condemned. - Mark 16:15-16

The LORD can give us visions and dreams and direct words of instruction—to our hearts, and through other people, books, music, movies, nature, circumstances, and more.

King Jesus will very soon return, and we are to be about His business!

What are we doing with what we know He has told us to do? Ask Him to speak to you in your dreams, and to help you understand when He is speaking to you in other ways. Of course, He will always speak to you through His Word, and He can help you understand things when you worship and pray. He hears your sincere prayers and answers!

Ask Him to speak to you about the call on your life; to show you the next step. He will!

Chapter 9: Reborn As Kings and Priests

B ut you are a chosen people, a royal priesthood, a holy nation, a people for God's own possession to proclaim the virtues of Him who called you out of darkness into His marvelous light. – I Peter 2:9

IN MY VISION, JESUS and I are in space, looking upon earth. He is huge.

As people get born again by receiving Christ Jesus as Savior and LORD, they are becoming part of the Kingdom of God, and instantly reborn as kings and priests of the Most High God.

From my perspective with Him in space, looking down at earth as a ball - like an astronaut would see it—the people that are being born again are coming through the nail hole in the LORD's huge hand, which is bigger than the world!

As the people who have chosen to be born again by receiving Him come through, I see them placed on thrones.

There is a constant line of people from the earth coming through His nail-pierced hand. *Hallelujah!*

This is truly His heart for us—that none would be lost; that all peoples (whom He created; Whom He alone gives every breath!) would come to Him, and be saved and healed and restored and blessed and protected and delighted and satisfied and more!

⁵ **...and from Jesus Christ, the faithful witness, the firstborn from the dead, and the ruler of the kings of the earth. To Him who loves us**

and has released us from our sins by His blood, ⁶who has made us to be a kingdom, priests to His God and Father—to Him be the glory and power forever and ever!

Amen.

⁷Behold, He is coming with the clouds, and every eye will see Him—even those who pierced Him. And all the tribes of the earth will mourn because of Him. So shall it be! Amen—Revelation 1:5-7

Chapter 10: Dance of Delight

" **Do not grieve, for the joy of the LORD is your strength,**" says
••• Nehemiah 8:10.

IN MY VISION, I AM a little girl, probably 3 or 4. My hair is long and dark blond, to my waist.

Jesus has picked me up and is holding me, dancing around in circles with me, and smiling and laughing.

We are together, and our joy is real, energizing, and sublime. We are delighting in just being together!

I learned a few years ago that the word Eden—as in Garden of Eden—means "delight." I know that is the original intent of our darling Daddy God, Jehovah (He becomes our Father when we receive His Son, the LORD Jesus Christ, as our Savior and LORD. John 3:15-17, Romans 3:23, 6:23, and 10:13)—to give us delight.

His will for us was and always is good and only good. He never intended for humans to have to suffer any bad! But Adam and Eve betrayed Him and listened to the enemy (the devil, who is the liar) instead, and brought curse into the world forever.

But Jesus! Jesus, the pure holy Son of God, came to restore us to the Father and the Father to us; He came to restore the delight of life to us!

When we choose to delight ourselves in the LORD, He gives us the desires and secret petitions of our hearts, says Psalm 37:4.

As true Believers in Christ Jesus, we long for our families—especially our children—to believe in and love and serve the LORD. Here is one promise the LORD gives us about that:

"Moreover the LORD your God will circumcise your heart and the heart of your descendants, to love the LORD your God with all your heart and with all your soul, so that you may live."- Deut. 30:6

If you would like to delight in the LORD and have Him truly delight in you, then you must be born again by receiving the LORD Jesus Christ, God's Son, as your Savior and LORD and Best Friend Forever! (Best friends delight in each other!).

Romans 10:9 says that if you will confess the LORD Jesus with your mouth and believe that God raised Him from the dead, then you will be saved (born again). Say the prayer at the beginning of this book and believe it with all your heart and watch your life change for the better.

If you have never danced before the LORD, now is the time to start! No worries if you feel weird; every new thing usually feels strange, at least at the beginning.

The LORD loves it when we dance freely before Him—even if we feel awkward. Ask Him to help you just be free. Sometimes, you have to simply choose to start dancing! If you ever did a "dance" at a school event, or a club, etc., then you can certainly dance to the LORD! It is an offering of praise, of worship, and a humbling thing. When we choose to thank and praise the LORD, it is an act of humility.

If Jesus, Who is God, can humble Himself and come to earth; live as a man and be tempted in every way but without sinning; be crucified for us on the cross—where He was separated from His Father, God!—and shed His pure blood to pay for all our sins; go to hell; then be raised again to new life after three days, then we can certainly do a little dance of thanksgiving in our living room! You may never dance at church, but do it at home to Him!

Chapter 11: Resting and Rejoicing in the LORD!

1 The LORD is my shepherd, I shall not want. 2 He makes me lie down in green pastures; He leads me beside quiet waters.

3 He restores my soul; He guides me in the paths of righteousness For His name's sake. – Psalm 23:1-3

IN THE FIRST PART OF my vision, my daughter is a little girl, about 3 or 4. I am a young adult. We are with Jesus, in a lovely, peaceful, grassy field, and all sitting—resting—on the ground.

He is smiling at us and holding a baby cottontail bunny, which is quiet in His nail-pierced hand, and letting us pet it.

In the second part of my vision, the LORD Jesus our Brother and Best Friend Forever is sitting in the same lovely grassy field. We are with Him.

My daughter (about the same age as the first part), and I are dancing around Him, delightfully happy and singing, and gently dropping pretty, white wildflowers in His hair. He smiles and enjoys it. What an awesome, wonderful, personal, gentle Savior we serve!

The LORD is good to all; His compassion rests on all He has made. - Psalm 145:9

Grace, mercy, and peace from God the Father and from Jesus Christ, the Son of the Father, will be with us in truth and love. - II John 1:3

Ask Him to show you how He sees you, as His precious child!

Chapter 12: Light Beings

A nd this is the message we have heard from Him and announce to you: God is light, and in Him there is no darkness at all. – I John 1:5

IN MY VISION, WHICH was very short and happened as my husband and I were walking into our home after a good church service, I saw my husband and myself riding horses.

This was unusual, because we did not do that, and had rarely been on such an animal in our childhoods.

The horses both started to fall on the ground. But we were not injured. As the horses lay on the ground, my husband and I both got up—then unzipped our "earth suits" (bodies)—so that our *true* selves could shine forth; indeed, we were, as is the LORD Jesus (I John 1:5), *pure Light*!

Then the vision ended.

This world system is dark—and getting darker. But the true Light of the Word of God, the LORD Jesus Christ (John 1:1-5), is the Light; the Way, the Truth, the Life.

Truly, Christ Jesus is the only Way to Heaven, the only Rescue from the evil and the mess of this failing world!

Jesus answered, "I am the way and the truth and the life. No one comes to the Father except through Me. - John 14:6

If you want new life; to escape the darkness and have a much better life, the God Life (called "Zoe," which means "life as God has it," - John

10:10), then you can call upon the Name of the LORD and be saved—born again into Christ Jesus!

If have not been born again and want to receive Christ Jesus (The Messiah) as your Savior, LORD, and Best Friend forever (He will never leave you nor forsake you! Hebrews 13:5), please say this quick prayer:

LORD Jesus, I choose to believe that You died for me to shed Your pure blood on the cross, and cleanse me from my sins; from all wrongs in my life. I choose to receive what You did for me, and I ask You to come into my life and be my Savior and LORD. I thank You that Your blood gives me the power to live the new Life You have given me (II Cor. 5:17). Please take my life and do something wonderful with it! Thank You, LORD Jesus!

Now, if you just said that prayer and meant it, you are truly born again! God is now your loving Father (I John 3:1), Jesus is your Brother Who and Good Shepherd who will always be with you and will lead you in right paths, and the angels are having a party to celebrate your most excellent decision (Luke 15:7)!

Your spirit has been translated from the temporary kingdom of darkness into the eternal Kingdom of Light of God's dear Son, King Jesus (Colossians 1:13, 14)!

Now, with Jesus Who is Love (I John 4:8), you are able to walk in Love toward God, yourself, and others!

For as the Word of God says in I John 2:9 and 10:9 says: **If anyone claims to be in the light but hates his brother, he is still in the darkness. 10 Whoever loves his brother remains in the light, and there is no cause of stumbling in him.**

Remember that you are, as a born-again child of God, a child of the Light (Truth; purity; revelation), not a child of the darkness (evil, the enemy, whatever is against God's Word).

8 For you were once darkness, but now you are light in the Lord. Walk as children of light, 9 for the fruit of the light consists in all goodness, righteousness, and truth. - Ephesians 5:8-9

Christ Jesus is faithful, true; totally dependable. There is no one like Him! He always means what He says in His Word, the Holy Bible, and says what He means. Praise Him!

Christ Jesus is the only absolute in the world. He is the Standard that people are looking for. He is Integrity and Excellence, Faithfulness and True Pure Love! Hallelujah!

Ask the LORD to reveal to you wherever the enemy has deceived you; ask the LORD to shed His light (revealing power; truth) upon those areas in your life that need to change, and to partner with Him to bring more light to and through your life, so you and others will experience Him more powerfully!

He loves you very much, and has been waiting for you. He will help you!

Chapter 13: Death of the Five-headed Snake

N ow the serpent was more crafty than any beast of the field that the LORD God had made. And he said to the woman, "Did God really say, 'You must not eat from any tree in the garden?'" - Genesis 3:1

And the great dragon was hurled down—that ancient serpent called the devil and satan, the deceiver of the whole world. He was hurled to the earth, and his angels with him. – Revelation 12:9

WHEN I FIRST CAME TO my current church (where I've been covered for almost 16 years, and where the pastor (apostle) married my husband and me over 14 years ago), I had a vision.

Our pastor had called us to the altar to take dominion over something I cannot remember now.

He was telling us to take a step (in reality), to "step over the snake at the door."

I obeyed, not understanding everything, but walking by faith in my God.

Suddenly, I had a vision: The snake at the threshold of the door of my life had *five* heads! Yuck phooey!

No wonder that—even though I knew I had been born again a couple decades earlier—I had had so much trouble in life—so much venom from so many (demonic) "snake bites"!

I had learned a few things once I'd become Spirit-filled a few years earlier; that snakes represented the evil one, who is the oppressor, suppressor and depressor—the one who works to bind us, to take away our freedom.

Also, five is the number of Grace, and the enemy always tries to counterfeit what God does.

So having five snakes should not have been a surprise, for the Grace of God was upon me to do His will in the earth—as it is on every true Believer!

Anyway, I knew that the LORD God Himself, the great Jehovah Nissi (Our victorious Miracle Banner, Exodus 17:15) had given me the Victory, for He is our Victory!

But thanks be to God, who gives us the victory through our Lord Jesus Christ! - I Corinthians 15:57

So, although I and anyone watching me could not see anything in the natural, I raised my arms as if they held a sword (for they certainly did, in the Spiritual realm!), and imagined me seeing a five-headed snake lying at my feet, as if reading to strike when I walked forward into the things of God.

But I took my sword in the Spirit (with Jehovah Nissi in me and with me) and slammed it down, severing the five heads from the body of that putrid, evil, defeated serpent!

Then I stepped over, taking a literal physical step into my new life!

17 Therefore if anyone is in Christ, he is a new creation. The old has passed away. Behold, the new has come! 18 All this is from God, who reconciled us to Himself through Christ and gave us the ministry of reconciliation: - II Corinthians 5:17-18

Then the vision ended, and my reality was released!

Much venom had been drained out of my life, and healing and restoration of those areas had come!

If you are tired and weary of being sick from snake venom—the evil of the enemy, that serpent, the defeated satan, whom the LORD Jesus

Christ totally whipped and stripped at the cross of Calvary—-then you need to be born again.

It is a rebirthing of your spirit!

Ask the LORD Jesus to reveal every "snake" in your life; to forgive you of your sins; to remove the venom from every snakebite of the enemy—and come into your heart and be your LORD and Savior.

Thank Him for dying on the cross for you, and for rising again to bring you to new life in Him (John 3:14-17)! Hallelujah!

He will come into your heart—*immediately*—and your life will be transformed on the inside. As you follow Him, your life will be transformed on the outside.

The more you get to know Him by reading the Bible, going to a Bible-teaching church, praying (talking to) the LORD, cultivating relationships with other true Believers, and worshiping Him to music that really glorifies Him, He will teach you His ways, and help you make changes that will give you more and more satisfaction, freedom, victory, and prosperity—which was His Plan all along, in the Garden of Eden (Genesis 1, 2)!

He is a patient, understanding, and gentle Savior, and loves you very much. He will help you every step of the way to know Him and love and serve Him—which will be the deepest delight of your life!

Chapter 14: The Dredge

Whoever invokes a blessing in the land will do so by the God of truth, and whoever takes an oath in the land will swear by the God of truth. For the former troubles will be forgotten and hidden from My sight. – Isaiah 65:16

WHEN A LEADER IN MY church asked me a simple question about my habits, I was surprised to find myself giving way too much information—some of it about the negative past, which was totally uncalled for. The LORD is so good and gracious! He gave me one word and a picture, and delivered me from the mess!

There were a couple of things that came out in the texts to the leader, a woman I greatly respect and connected immediately with when I met her, that I knew meant that there were still some ties to the past.

So, the LORD is so good. The Holy Spirit of Truth knows all things about us, for all time—even every word before it's on our tongues! How truly awesome is our God, the LORD Jesus Christ, Elohim, Who is Jehovah; the Sovereign LORD—God alone! Hallelujah!

Here's what the good, good LORD did for me, and He will do for you what YOU need, in the moment of your need—if you will humble yourself and ask for and receive His help!

He is our loving Father (when we truly have repented of our sins and chosen to believe and receive what His pure blood did when He sacrificed Himself on the cross, over 2,000 years ago—all for us, that we would be delivered from this evil world, and have peace and safety and abundance on the earth, and a perfect eternal Heavenly home with the LORD when our bodies die! Hallelujah!).

So the LORD gave me one word in my heart and mind: "Dredge."

I thought I knew what a dredge was, and I was right, when I checked with an online dictionary. With that word, He gave me the picture of Himself, as a Director of construction. Jesus my Savior, my Deliverer, my Helper, the Living Word, was dressed in work clothes, including a hardhat and spiked boots.

He was smiling at me. Hallelujah!

He looked up at me. I was in a big, red, enclosed crane-like machine, much taller than Him as He stood on the ground. It was the equipment I needed to dredge—to dig down into and scoop up to clean out the putrid "pond", the slimy slough, in front of me—which I knew held the snakes, and squids and eels, and other revolting creatures that represented the wrong things in my soul.

So, He smiled and waved at me, to go ahead. I took the control, and moved the dredge to start scooping.

As I dredged up the slimy, squirming, creepy things that represented my sins and wrong thoughts; lies I'd agreed with, and more, I made them land in front of my Savior, Jehovah Nissi. He immediately started beheading and/or crushing these wrong things. Hallelujah!

The God of peace will soon crush Satan under your fee. The grace of our Lord Jesus Christ be with you. – Romans 16:20

It took three times to get all the junk dredged out. Yuck phooey, but so worth it!

The best part is that, the whole time, Jesus was smiling at me!

He grimaced while He killed and crushed the wrong things, but, when He looked at me, every time, He was smiling!

He is such a gracious Savior! He is for us, and none can be against us!

What then shall we say in response to these things? If God is for us, who can be against us? - Romans 8:31

Then my LORD directed me to scoop up all the dead bodies of the past, in gross groups and heaps, and sling them into the Sea of Forgetfulness, which sparkled just beyond the pond of old.

I did, and felt so much lighter! He has made me glad!

Do not call to mind the former things, Or ponder things of the past. "Behold, I will do something new, Now it will spring forth; Will you not be aware of it? I will even make a roadway in the wilderness, Rivers in the desert." – Isaiah 43:18-19

God is ready to do new things in your life. First—just like we clear out our closets and other storage places, to make room for other things—you may need to clean out some old things.

Will you let Him help you today?

His plans for you are more exciting and fulfilling than you can know! (I'm preaching to myself too!)

For we are God's workmanship, created in Christ Jesus to do good works, which God prepared in advance as our way of life. – Ephesians 2:10

We'll never go wrong following the LORD!

Then, once you are cleansed by the LORD's help, ask Him to fill you freshly with Himself, with His Holy Spirit, and to teach you to yield to Him, so that He can express Himself more through you, and others will see more of Christ and be drawn to Him—which is why we true Believers are on the planet!

He will, and you will be thrilled!

To them God has chosen to make known among the Gentiles the glorious riches of this mystery, which is Christ in you, the hope of glory. – Colossians 1:27

CHRIST IN US, the HOPE OF GLORY!

HALLELUJAH!!

Chapter 15: The Door to the Past Slams Shut

A nd when He comes, He will convict the world in regard to sin and righteousness and judgment: - John 16:8

IN THE VISION, MY HUSBAND and I had repented to God and each other about some things that needed to be corrected.

We took Communion (I Corinthians 10:16) over the old junk being defeated and gone; us being healed from that old wrong thinking and acting, it to seal it in our hearts and the Spirit.

As Isaiah 43:18 and 19 state: **18 "Do not call to mind the former things, Or ponder things of the past. 19 "Behold, I will do something new, Now it will spring forth; Will you not be aware of it? I will even make a roadway in the wilderness, Rivers in the desert."**

We must choose to forgive, forget, and move on. At that moment, we were choosing to do all of that.

Suddenly, I had a flash of a stone wall in which was an old wooden round-top gate or door. The gate had vines and things on it, and I *saw and heard* it swing *shut*, with a victorious finality—for it would *never* be opened again!

13 Brethren, I do not regard myself as having laid hold of it yet; but one thing I do: forgetting what lies behind and reaching forward to what lies ahead, 14 I press on toward the goal for the prize of the upward call of God in Christ Jesus. — Philippians 3:13-14)

If your life has been a mess, know this: Only Jesus Christ can fix it, and He can not only fix it; He can do miracles for you!

And He wants to! All you have to do is agree to receive Him as your Savior, LORD, and best Friend (He's the Best!). He did all the hard work at Calvary, where He paid the full terrible price by shedding His pure blood for all your sins and mine, so we could be free to have an abundant life (Zoe; "life as God has it"; John 10:10)!

Sometimes, more than we know, hurts and harms from the past can truly hinder us from being happy, peaceful, creative, productive, and more. Many times, the hurts and harms are so deep, that we must have the power of God to truly free us from these things and bring healing.

Ask the LORD to help you find the right Bible-believing church with a pastor that truly follows Him; to find the Scriptures that apply to your specific situations to speak over yourself; to lead you to worship songs infused with His Spirit that will being healing to your soul as you sing along; and to help you pray (talk to) Him about your situations—which includes forgiving those that have hurt you, and even God and yourself! He will!

Chapter 16: Hearts Are Born in His Praise

2 to proclaim Your loving devotion in the morning and Your faithfulness at night 3 with the ten-stringed harp and the melody of the lyre. 4 For You, O LORD, have made me glad by Your deeds; I sing for joy at the works of Your hands. – Psalm 92:2-3

IN MY VISION, I SAW the LORD Jesus, sitting at a white baby grand piano, with a lovely sheen of mother-of pearl rainbow on it.

Jesus Himself was playing it! Music notes I could see rose into the air as He played—and there was a person in each note!

I don't know if this is before or after I taught Piano Lab to 5 and 6 graders at a large public school; the bulletin board idea from the LORD was a grand piano with music notes rising from it—and on each note was the name of a student. Each 9 weeks, I had 85 or so. So I taught over 320 to read, play, and perform piano music.

When I was 13, I started teaching private piano lessons, after having had lessons for years and being able to play successfully. Teaching is one of my gifts.

But the vision I had was glorious! Jesus is all about people, and He definitely is The Master Musician! All music that glorifies God comes from Him!

I believe this vision was to remind me that, when i play, it is really Him playing through me, and touching people with His music.

I believe it is possible, when He anoints anyone to play with His Spirit, that the hearts of many can literally be born again by His touch through the music that worships Him!

Although many around the world make motions of "worship" to their gods, there is only One God—Yahweh, the LORD Jesus Christ—and we can only truly worship Him with His Spirit helping our hearts.

Ask the LORD to teach you new ways to worship Him, like "spirit songs"—songs that are just between you and Him, for the moment; songs that can give you breakthroughs and other victories, for the LORD inhabits the praises of His people! (Psalm 22:3)

Chapter 17: Resting in the Arms of Jesus

The eternal God is your dwelling place, and underneath are the everlasting arms. He drives out the enemy from before you, giving the command, 'Destroy him!' - Deuteronomy 33:27

THROUGH THE YEARS, I often struggled with falling asleep, because thoughts of fear or frustration would keep me awake.

I was not obeying the Word, which says to "humble yourself and cast all your cares on Him, for He cares for you."

But the good LORD helped me start envisioning my wonderful LORD Jesus, waiting for me in a lovely garden, which was part of the outward courts of the Temple in Heaven.

I would envision myself as a little girl, about 5 years old. I would run up to Jesus, Who was smiling at me, and He'd pick me up in His strong loving arms.

It was just me and Him. He would hug me close, and hold me as a daddy holds his little girl.

Then I would quickly fall asleep, my head on His strong shoulder, and I would be perfectly at peace, resting in His arms.

The LORD appeared to us in the past, saying: "I have loved you with an everlasting love; therefore I have drawn you with loving devotion." – Jeremiah 31:3

True rest, true peace, can only come by being born again into the eternal Kingdom of Light; the Kingdom of God's dear Son, where Jesus Christ is Savior and LORD.

The LORD loves us so much! He is the perfect Parent, and wants us—even commands us—to rest. Ultimately, trusting Him is the true rest for our souls (mind, will, emotions; Hebrews 4:2-3).

Chapter 18: The Faithful and True Returns!

Then I saw heave standing open, and there before me was a white horse. And its rider is called Faithful and True. With righteousness He judges and wages war. – Revelation 19:11

SOMETHING I ENVISIONED years ago was a huge print on a sheet or some kind of light-weight cloth, to represent the moment that KING JESUS returns. It had thick, billowy clouds, and the strong muscled chest and front legs of the magnificent white horse on which our Majesty rode the edge of His robe dipped in blood, and His thigh reading *KING of kings and LORD of lords* (Rev. 19:16), with His legs and boots revealed...

The picture was one of intense anticipation, as if the horse with our LORD, Faithful and True, had just broken through—and then in the next moment we would *see Jesus*!

As King Jesus states in His Word, the Holy Bible: **"Behold, I am coming soon, and My reward is with Me, to give to each one according to what he has done. 13 I am the Alpha and the Omega, the First and the Last, the Beginning and the End."** – Revelation 22:12-13

Are you ready for the return of King Jesus? When the LORD returns, He is so good that He will give us credit when we "are found doing" (His will)! Hallelujah!

Jesus said that He delighted to do God's will (Psalm 40:8) and that to finish God's work was His food (John 4:34). It is ours as well!

Chapter 19: Christ is The Tree of Life

24 but to those who are the called, both Jews and Greeks, Christ the power of God and the wisdom of God. 25 Because the foolishness of God is wiser than men, and the weakness of God is stronger than men. – I Corinthians 1:24-25

DURING THIS VISION I had of the Tree of Life, while our New Year's Eve service continued into the wee hours the pastor mentioned that we were like trees, tapping into the water.

My vision was of my husband and myself, melded as one tree, with our daughter (then 15) fused into us. She was in the middle of us, surrounded by us, protected by us.

The tree that we were was not a giant oak. However, it was like the giant tree I saw in 1998. It was reported to be 1000 years old and mammoth and solid and thick—looking like a baobab tree. So we were—and are—a type of the Tree of Life, for Jesus is in us because we have believed in Him.

As huge as the tree was, Jesus is bigger. He *is* the Tree of Life, for He is Wisdom, and the Word says in Proverbs 3:18 that (Wisdom) **"She is a tree of life to those who embrace her, and those who lay hold of her are blessed."**

The LORD tells us in James 1:5 that, when we ask, He will give us abundant wisdom. He also promises in Isaiah 33:6 to give us stability—like a well-established tree—in our time. Hallelujah!

5 The LORD is exalted... the stability of your times, A wealth of salvation, wisdom and knowledge...– Isa.33:5-6

Chapter 20: The Word Lifts Me To Lift Him!

"And I, when I am lifted up from the earth, will draw everyone to Myself." – John 12:32

THE LORD GAVE ME THIS glorious vision during Communion at church, on Resurrection Day 2022. As our pastor, an apostle and prophet, preached to us that the old us died with Christ and the new us was risen with Him—that the new us is *risen indeed*--I saw the LORD Jesus. He lifted me up. I stood on His nail-pierced hands!

I was dressed in a lovely white satin and silk suit, and I held a huge gleaming sword. LORD Jesus lifted me up and I lifted high the sword to the sky—where Father God reached down with His lightnings of power!

14 "As Moses lifted up the serpent in the wilderness, even so must the Son of Man be lifted up; 15 so that whoever believes will in Him have eternal life. 16 "For God so loved the world, that He gave His only begotten Son, that whoever believes in Him shall not perish, but have eternal life. 17 "For God did not send the Son into the world to judge the world, but that the world might be saved through Him. – John 3:14-17

The Word lifted me up to lift up the Word to the world!

Ask the LORD to show you new ways to exalt Him to the world. He will!

Chapter 21: I Am His Bride!

Let us rejoice and be glad and give Him the glory. For the marriage of the Lamb has come, and His bride has made herself ready .– Revelation 19:7

DURING A POWERFUL CLASS at my church, we invited the Holy Spirit to speak to us in a way that would assure us that He was with us.

I was so touched at the vision He gave me, that I wept silent tears of joy!

In the vision, I was a young, joyful bride, radiant with thanksgiving and anticipation, dressed in a gloriously elegant wedding gown, with a very long train! I was in a huge, cathedral-style church, with stained glass windows and extremely high, ornate ceilings.

There were hundreds of people in the pews.

My train was held by my daughter, about four years old, and she was happy about it.

I was walking up to my royal bridegroom—Who was the LORD Jesus Himself, tall and handsome, dressed in the white military uniform of an officer! He wore His officer's hat, and He was beaming at me, with eyes so loving and deep.

I was amazed and overwhelmed and totally thrilled, as I thought, *I am His Bride!*

The vision was only a few seconds, but was very powerful, very real.

The LORD will do the same for you! Ask the Holy Spirit, Who is God, Who loves and knows you better than you know yourself, to speak to you in a way that you *know* that He is communicating with you, even if you don't hear words. He will!

As a true Believer—one who has asked the LORD's forgiveness of all your sins, and for Christ Jesus to come into your heart and be your Savior and LORD (and constant Companion and Friend!)—*you are the Bride of Christ!*

One night the Lord spoke to Paul in a vision: "Do not be afraid; keep on speaking; do not be silent." – Acts 18:9

That which was from the beginning, which we have heard, which we have seen with our own eyes, which we have gazed upon and touched with our own hands—this is the Word of life. – I John 1:1

⤳⧜⤶

The End of *Visions of the King: Jesus Revealed*

Don't miss out!

Visit the website below and you can sign up to receive emails whenever Tonja K. Taylor publishes a new book. There's no charge and no obligation.

https://books2read.com/r/B-A-HSCAB-RBEQG

BOOKS 2 READ

Connecting independent readers to independent writers.

Did you love *Visions of the King: Jesus Revealed*? Then you should read *Spirit Songs & Stories Enhanced #2*[1] by Tonja K. Taylor et al.!

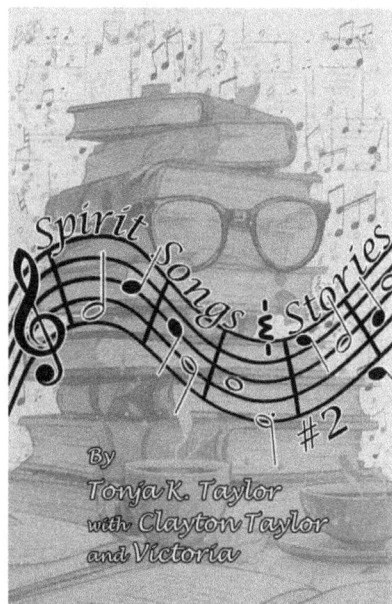

From **horses to angels to eagles**; to a true humorous **homeschooling adventure** with a Siamese Fighting Fish, along with **detailed footnotes** for learning fun; instruction and examples on **how to write songs and poetry**; three **bilingual (Spanish-English) works**; a customizable **holiday craft project**, in addition to original Christmas poems to share; several **excerpts from The Adventures of Princess Pearl, P.O.W.E.R. (Purposeful Operations With Eternal Rewards) Girl!**; ATOS levels for every piece; and **questions to strengthen and expand critical thinking** skills, **Tonja K. Taylor's** collection of delightful and insightful originals for **grade 6 and up** feature **meaningful, moral, and thought-provoking stories, songs, and poems** (including three by

---

1. https://books2read.com/u/bzNoG9

2. https://books2read.com/u/bzNoG9

Tonja's husband). Her creative works enrich and empower her readers, as they enjoy experiencing **higher levels of knowledge and engagement**; literary right and might!

Also by Tonja K. Taylor

POWERLight Lit Tips for Better Teaching
The New Legacy Expanded
P.O.W.E.R. Princess Poetry Plus
The Adventures of Princess Pearl, P.O.W.E.R. Girl!
Your Holy Health: Effective Secrets to Divine Life
Spirit Songs & Stories Enhanced
Spirit Songs & Stories Enhanced #2
Visions of the King: Jesus Revealed

Watch for more at https://www.faithwriters.com/
member-profile.php?id=64826.

About the Author

Tonja K. Taylor loves to help others know the LORD Jesus Christ, through her creative communications; writing, service, presentations, and more.

Her decades of championing children in school, church, and community, plus her experience in business, the fine arts, ministry, and other arenas, has equipped her to bring a multi-faceted approach to her work.

Tonja's audiences learn many useful and interesting things, providing them with an amazing amount of value for their investment, while they strengthen their creativity and critical thinking skills.

She and her husband enjoy helping others know the Savior, the soon-returning King!

Read more at https://www.faithwriters.com/member-profile.php?id=64826.

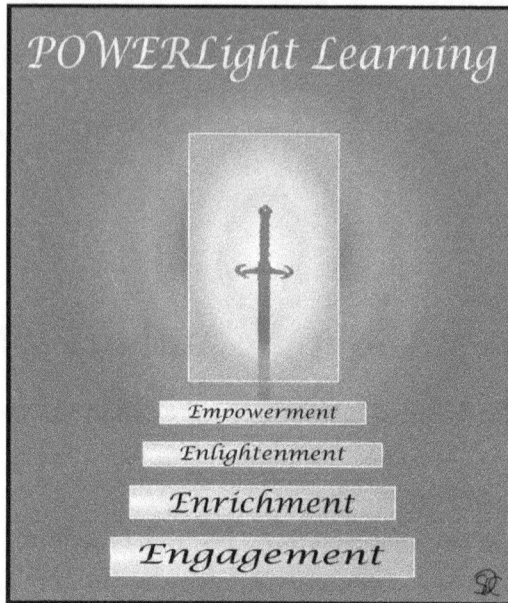

POWERLight Learning

Empowerment
Enlightenment
Enrichment
Engagement

About the Publisher

"Do not be conformed to this world, but be transformed by the renewing of your mind. Then you will be able to test and approve what is the good, pleasing, and perfect will of God." - Romans 12:2, Berean Standard Bible

POWERLight Learning exists to produce writings and other creative works that engage, enrich, empower, and enlighten others about how the importance of what they experience influences their lives, and the lives of many others!

Read more at https://www.faithwriters.com/member-profile.php?id=64826.